KEEPER OF THE PIPE

By
John Inman

As told to
Vickie Leigh Krudwig

JUNIPER WINDS PRESS, INC.

Library of Congress Cataloging-in-Publication Data
Keeper of the Pipe: includes the true story of
John Inman and his extraordinary find-a stone Ute pipe.

LCCN# 20044117069
ISBN 0-9700127-4-8
1.Non-fiction, 2. biography, 3. Indians of North America,
4. Western history, 5. Colorado History

First Printing December 1, 2004
ISBN – 0-9700127-4-8
Printed in Denver, Colorado

Produced and distributed by

JUNIPER WINDS PRESS, INC.
10012 Bryant Court
Federal Heights, CO 80260
(303) 469-2223
(800) 256-1310 #01

Keeper of the Pipe

Dedicated to the spirit of the Ute people and all the others who have guided me along the journey of life, making everyday a learning experience.

J. I.

Dedicated to my dear friend, John Inman, and to his family. Thank you for your friendship and for sharing your amazing history with me.

V. K.

"When you see a new trail, or a footprint you do not know, follow it to the point of knowing."

Uncheedah
The grandmother of Ohiyesa

Keeper of the Pipe

TABLE OF CONTENTS

A NOTE FROM JOHN INMAN

This is my story, this is my tale. I tried to put things in to sequence as our life unfolded in the lower Coal Creek Valley. I have touched on the high points of our life here as they happened. Yet, it is the small, simple things that made my life's road trip so blessed.

One does not need to look at things through "rosy eyeballs" due to alcohol or drugs to feel blessed by the great Creation. Of all things great or small, hugs, smiles, kind words and harmless jokes are some of life's greatest moments. It is with this spirit that I share these recollections with you.

Along the way I have lost parents, grandparents, siblings, aunts, uncles, cousins and friends. But I have their pictures and memories to remind me of happier times. Someday, I suppose, I too will be but a memory.

If I could, I would like to hang around for another hundred years to see what happens to the technology this generation leaves behind. Will the next generation improve it? Will they use it to destroy creation or worse yet, mankind? Though an old adage claims "we've come a long way, baby," I often wonder where we are going.

Keeper of the Pipe

INTRODUCTION

In the quiet hours of the nighttime, it was a Ute custom for the men of the band to gather together after their evening meal, discuss the day's events, and to talk about plans for their future. It was during this time that the host would remove his beaded pipe bag from its resting place and offer his visitors tobacco in a gesture of peace and friendship. Shoulder to shoulder in the warmth and glow of the campfire light, the men recounted their hunting experiences and told stories about the past.

For me it is easy to imagine Ouray, the Tabeguache leader, as he carefully picked up his beaded pipe bag and removed his old granite pipe. His fellow tribesmen watched in silence as their host carefully joined the sacred stone pipe bowl and its stem together. Then reaching into his tobacco bag, Ouray pulled out a few of the dried leaves and rubbed them carefully between his hands. Once satisfied, he loaded the crushed tobacco into the stone bowl of his pipe and tamped it down carefully.

As the fire crackled, Ouray picked up a long stick and placed it into the fire. It was from the warmth of his hearth that he lit the stone pipe. Ouray closed his eyes and lifted the pipe upwards, offering the sacred tobacco to Creator and to the Four Sacred Directions. Then Ouray put the pipe stem to his mouth and drew his breath in. The men in the teepee nodded in satisfaction as Ouray exhaled. Wisps of gray smoke rose up into the night air and to the ancestors. Their prayers had been heard. The pipe was passed in a clockwise direction to each man in the teepee (being careful not to let the pipe cross the doorway). Once everyone had smoked the pipe it was returned to Ouray.

A long time ago, according to the Ute customs, the only time a woman smoked the pipe is when she was a Shaman. Young boys earned the right to smoke the tobacco pipe after they proved themselves by killing game and fighting their enemies. When the time finally came, young boys gathered outside the teepee of a tribal leader and sang. They beat a rawhide or hand drum and sang their songs until they were invited into the teepee to smoke with the men.

Pipes like these were used during all of the treaty talks between the Ute leaders and the United States Government. The pipes were passed around to members of the delegation to set the intention of peace throughout the talks. Ouray, like many other leaders, participated in numerous treaty talks. The passing of the Ute pipe was a crucial part of the peacemaking process, and today, tobacco pipes are still considered important part of the Ute culture. Prayers of the People still rise with the smoke to the long gone ancestors of yesterday, yet their memories and their stories are remembered with the passing of the pipe.

Ute pipes were sometimes made of clay, or of a red rock found near Provo and Duchesne, Utah, and in a few other unidentified places. The bowls were carefully shaped and then hollowed out using a spear or arrow point. The long wooden stem of the pipe was often made of elder or wild rose wood stems and was eight to fifteen inches long.

The soft interior of the stems were pushed out using another stick.

Some Ute pipes were made of hardened stone found in the Rocky Mountains, their stems being made from hollow reeds. These stone pipes were not shaped like some of the Native American tobacco pipes you see today; their shape was similar to the modern day corn-cob pipe.

Tobacco was not only used for pleasure, it was, and still is, a sacred plant of the People. It is the wispy rising smoke of the burning tobacco that carries prayers to the ancestors in the Spirit World and to the Creator. Wild tobacco grew plentifully in the wilderness. The leaves were harvested in the fall and laid in the sun to dry, then placed into buckskin bags.

Sometimes other plants such as kinnikinic were added to the tobacco mixture. Kinnikinic, which grew abundantly in the rocky and sandy slopes of the mountains and hillsides, and in forested areas, was often used by miners and settlers when they ran out of tobacco.

It's amazing to think that the pipe seen on page 36 was once carried by Shavano, and perhaps smoked by the great Ute leader Ouray. It's even more fantastic to know that a six year old boy, so long ago discovered such an object and that he kept his word to Ouray to take care of the pipe. It is in this spirit that we pass John's story, *Keeper of the Pipe* on to you.

CHAPTER ONE
The Move West

With one brown eye, and the other a startling blue, I was born July 4, 1926—number six in the family. I was the fifth surviving child, as one brother died shortly after his birth. My mother, Viola Mae Inman, always told me that an old buzzard laid an egg on a rock out in Red River, and that the sun hatched me out of it.

My father, John Inman, Sr. worked at the rock quarry on Red River, which was located a short distance from Heber City, Arkansas. We left there after a tornado hit Heber Springs and destroyed our home. What didn't blow away, burned up. I was never able to get a birth certificate because of the fire. Shortly after the tornado, our family moved to Oklahoma where my father worked in the oil fields.

Our family, like many others, faced unpredictable times as the United States was experiencing a great financial upheaval. Banks and businesses shut down in record numbers and many people found themselves without work or food.

John Inman, Sr. and his wife Viola, just before
their move to Colorado (Courtesy of John Inman).

To make matters worse, the states in the Midwest were in the throes of a long drought. Millions of grasshoppers swarmed over the lands, devouring everything in their paths. There was little anyone could do. Struggling farmers had no choice but to leave their traditional farmsteads for employment opportunities in nearby cities and towns.

Even though my father had a job, he decided to move our family to the lower Coal Creek Valley, west of Montrose, Colorado. In 1928, when I was two years old, my parents loaded our belongings into my father's new Model-T Ford truck. After saying goodbye to friends and neighbors, we headed west to join my uncle Robert and his family on their farm in Montrose.

The drive west was a long and difficult process. My parents were accustomed to long, flat stretches of highway on the open prairies. They were unfamiliar with mountain driving. To make life more interesting, my father's truck had no brakes. If a person wanted to slow their vehicle down, or stop, they had to step on the reverse pedal (located next to the gas pedal).

This unique braking process required my father to stop several times on our trip west. He had to constantly replace the "reverse bands" on the truck, as the bands wore out quickly on the steep slopes of the Rocky Mountains. These reverse bands looked like lamp wick to me. My father bought the material in a great big roll. Each time the band wore out; he would stop the truck, and repeat the process of replacing the worn bands. He would cut off what was needed and replace it as trip progressed.

Once, my father pulled the car off to the side of the road to replace the reverse band. He saw a small mound and thought the site would be a safe place to park the car. He lay down on the mound and began to work on the truck. Suddenly, father jumped up. We watched as he quickly began to stomp his feet and slap at his body. The mound, it seemed, was an anthill! The discontented red ants swarmed over my father's body. They let him know that his stopover was unwelcome.

Cochetopa Pass made everyone anxious. The road seemed too steep for driving. When we reached the summit, mother asked father to stop the car. Even though she was pregnant, mother refused to ride in the Model-T as it made its way down the steep inclines. Without brakes, mother wasn't going to take chances!

While father and my older brothers drove down the steep hill, I walked with my mother, brothers and sisters. Because I was only two at the time, my older sister carried me on her hip as we safely made our way to the bottom. Once we reached the base of the mountain, we climbed back into the Model-T and continued on our way to Uncle Robert's.

As we drove into Montrose, our eyes scanned the horizon. Mother and father smiled at one another while the children chattered excitedly. We had finally arrived at our new home! The breathtaking view of Montrose could hardly compare to the stark and dusty landscape of Oklahoma and Arkansas. Here there was no Dustbowl. Water from the Uncompahgre River flowed slowly across the countryside, creating vast stretches of rich river bottom lands. Horses and small herds of sheep and cows grazed contently on the grasses, while magpies and crows flew overhead, scolding one another.

The shimmering leaves on the enormous cottonwood trees along the river banks were beginning to turn yellow. Apple orchards lay scattered across the city of Montrose, painting the landscape with many shades of green, red and copper. Seas of gold and umber grasses grew along the roadside and rustled softly in the light autumn breeze.

Change was in the cool crisp air, and with it, the expectation of a new and unfamiliar way of life for our family. Hope and the promise of good things to come had carried our family thousands of miles across the parched prairies of America. We had arrived safely and my parents rejoiced at the thought.

It wasn't long before we settled comfortably into my uncle Robert's house. Lucky for us, we had arrived just in time. Shortly after our arrival, on Halloween night, my mother gave birth to my baby brother, Bobby Gene. He was the first Inman to be born in our new home in Montrose, Colorado.

This was the beginning of many happy memories in Montrose. Our family soon settled into life in the valley, changing with seasons as did the Ute Indians who once called this region home. Like these ancient Ute ancestors, we too would learn to appreciate the valley's rugged beauty. We understood their respect for the land and for its ability to sustain us during the hard times ahead.

We grew our crops in the rich fertile soils of the valley. Our family was grateful for the land, for the Creator's bounty. It was a time when our families watched out for each other. My cousins and I thrived in this setting. The Coal Creek Valley had soon become a permanent and unforgettable part of our long history.

The Old Pepper home in Coal Creek Valley (Photo courtesy of John Inman)

CHAPTER TWO
Pepper Gardens
A Home of Our Own

I was three years old when we finally moved into a home of our own. By 1929 there were several vacant houses in the valley. The Great Depression had devastating effects on many people living there. Banks had foreclosed on individuals who were unable to work and pay their bills. My family moved into a two-room log house with a lean-to kitchen. It was located on Franklin Mesa just south of Robert's home in the lower Coal Creek Valley. It wasn't fancy, but it was home!

In 1930, mother gave birth to my sister, Elvie Mae. Our growing family soon moved into a two-story house located under a hill in the Coal Creek Valley. Unfortunately, we did not reside there for long. The house had been sold. What was our family going to do? It was wintertime and we had no place to go.

Luckily for us, the new owner of the property welcomed us into his home for the long winter months. Our family lived in the house's upper story while the new

Father built the pig pen near a natural spring just west of the Pepper home. (Courtesy of Vickie Leigh Krudwig)

owner resided on the first floor. We were truly grateful for his generosity.

In the spring of 1931, when I was five years old, we moved into the old "Pepper Home" at the old "Peppers Gardens Farm" in the Coal Creek Valley. The old stone house sat west of Uncle Robert's house, and we were glad to settle there.

The old Pepper Home sat on 80 acres of land, with several out buildings used for storage and animals. The site of the home was perfect for a family with children. My parents happily moved in, with the hopes of purchasing the land for $3,500. We quickly settled in, and began establishing our own farm.

We purchased chickens and pigs. I watched as father built the pig's pen. He had selected an area around a natural spring just west of our new house. Father said the soggy ground was perfect for a hog wallow. Once the structure was complete, my parents purchased some hogs. The animals loved their new pen. They rooted in the wet soil for hours, and grew fatter with each passing day. Like many other farmers, we were delighted at their enormous size. The animals would provide us with meat later on.

Finally we had a place to call our own. Much to our dismay though, we lived within walking distance to the Coal Creek School in District 16. During the day, my siblings and I attended school where we learned reading, writing and yes, arithmetic. After classes, we all pitched in to complete countless daily chores that included feeding the hogs.

By age seven I was put in charge of our neighbor's "gentle giants," a small herd of Holstein cows. In exchange for my services, our family was supplied with fresh milk and cream for butter. Each day the cows waited for me to come. They bawled loudly in anticipation of their daily walk. There were times when those loud moos startled me!

With willow switch in hand, in the early afternoon light, I herded these massive animals down the road. There the cows grazed on the fresh green grasses growing along the roadsides. On weekends, I herded the cows down the road to nearby fields. I'd spend the day watching over them as the creatures fed on the grasses. While the cows grazed, I explored the natural world around me.

I studied ants and beetles as they ate and went about their work. Once I even resorted to borrowing my sister's tweezers without asking. I had used them to gather up ants and bugs and put them into jars. I loved to watch them as they crawled around inside. There was hardly a time when I didn't have a lizard or a frog in my pocket. These were happy times for a boy of seven!

In addition to taking care of the animals, my cousins, brothers, sisters and I had other chores to do. During the summer months, under bright sunny skies, we walked barefoot in a vivid green ocean, hand picking green beans. We learned how to harvest seed onions from the land, too. Once the onions were picked, we laid them on the roof of Uncle Robert's root cellar where the vegetables could dry in the sunlight. The onions would be ready for use in the following year. It was hard work, but the effort was well worth it.

Even though the effects of the Depression had been felt across the country, and money was tight, our families thrived. The crops and livestock kept our growing broods well fed and healthy. We were thankful for the nourishment we received from the Earth. Life in the lower Coal Creek Valley was good!

CHAPTER THREE
Cantaloupe Pie and Purple Teeth

Even though farm life was hard work, our family enjoyed many happy times there. One of our greatest tools for survival was having a good sense of humor. Laughter lightened our work loads, and the camaraderie we shared with one another made life more enjoyable.

There was the time when my Aunt Zola planted cantaloupe in her garden. Soon the sweet, juicy melons were ripe and ready for harvest. My aunt loved making pumpkin pies, and she figured the melons would be perfect for pies, too! Needless to say, her cantaloupes pies did not impress anyone. The pies were a disaster! I know that everyone teased my aunt about her cantaloupe pies for the rest of her life.

It seemed as though we were constantly moving. Shortly after my sister's birth, we moved to a two-story house just below a hill in Coal Creek Valley. Although my parents had moved into the old "I. L. Pepper Home" with the intention of purchasing the house, we were forced to move once again.

My father, who never liked to take chances, took too long to make the decision. While he considered the

Million Dollar Highway in 1920 . (Courtesy of Denver Public Library, Western History Collection, L. C. McClure, Call# MCC-3058)

purchase, my cousin, who had married a local girl from the valley, purchased the place with help from his father-in-in law. My folks eventually moved out in the fall of 1932.

By the time I started school in September 1932, my parents had moved into an old log house located in Shavano Valley. The land featured a large spring in the yard, north of the house. It provided our family with cool, sweet drinking water. Mother had another baby, and my father was working on the Million Dollar Highway between Ouray and Silverton. My two older brothers, Dan and Charles worked for the Colorado Conservation Corp (CCC) too.

The Depression was awful and many men desperately needed work. The CCC and the Million Dollar Highway jobs were created by President ~~Theodore~~ Roosevelt to help boost the economy. *FRANKLIN*

Because of the time of year, it was decided that my sister Elsie and I would stay with my cousin and his wife, "Ina" so we could attend school until spring of the following year. We stayed in the room at the north side of my cousin's house. During the school day, my sister rode into town with my ~~Aunt~~ Ina, who had a job there.

While my sister attended high school, I attended classes at Coal Creek Valley School. It was within walking distance from my cousin's house. Once school was dismissed for the summer, I spent most of my time exploring the foothills in the vicinity, finding arrowheads and artifacts.

I also played house with a little neighbor girl named "Dorothy." It was during this time that I learned that little girls were different from little boys, and I experienced my first kiss. Little girls wore bloomers with big letters across the seat that said, "Home Pride" or they had big

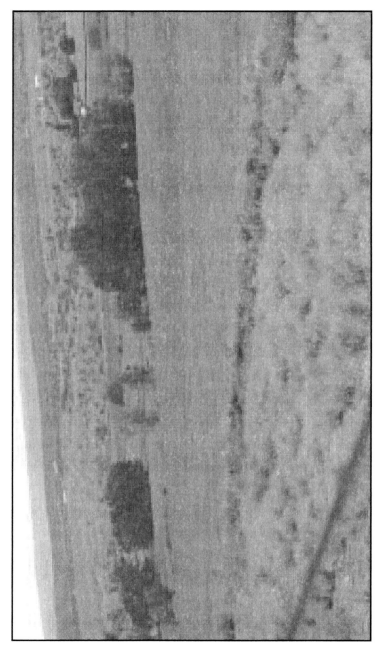

Coal Creek Valley near John's house. (Courtesy of Vickie Leigh Krudwig)

flowers on them. The bloomers, made from old flour sacks, had been designed by loving mothers.

I, like many other little boys, ran around in striped overalls, given to us by the Department of Welfare. Life in the valley seemed normal to me. Kids were getting measles, mumps, chicken pox, whooping cough and all kinds of "good things."

It was the time, too when people had purple teeth! In order to support the farmers in our area, the United States Government began to buy up surplus potatoes and onions from local farmers. The great quantities of produce was hauled to a nearby gulch and dumped out!

Government workers then poured non-toxic purple dye all over the vegetables to discourage local residents from eating them. Their plan didn't work. Starving families hastily gathered up the discolored produce. They took the vegetables home to eat, staining their teeth purple!

Most families in the valley did not own refrigerators. They kept coolers in the irrigation ditches, where the flowing water kept the food inside them cold. Most of our farms were heated by wood burning cook stoves and pot-bellied heaters. Electricity had not come to the valley yet.

We all lived simply then. In addition to planting and picking green beans and onions, my brother and I hoed corn, stacked hay and helped raise the big garden that my mother had planted. Each year my mother would can 1,200 to 1,400 quarts of fruit and vegetables. This would keep us well fed through the long winter months.

At Christmas, my parents could afford very little. With a large family and the Great Depression in full swing, the holidays were meager, yet joyful times. We celebrated the season by giving each other homemade presents. Sometimes as a special treat, father would go into the town of Olathe to buy a few precious gifts. If we were lucky,

Christmas, Montrose. (Courtesy of Denver Public Library, Western History Collection, photographer unknown, Call # X-10451)

we might get a pencil and a Big Chief tablet or even a box of crayons!

Even though times were tough, they were a time of connecting with the people in our neighborhood. I remember the time when a kind-hearted neighbor drove down the road with his wagon. It was loaded with firewood and fresh deer meat. He stopped along the way to share his "wealth" with his friends and family members living nearby. These kind acts are just a few of the examples of how our neighbors watched out for each other, and how we survived the Depression.

When I was in the first grade, I walked almost two miles to school. I had no coat to keep me warm during the colder weather. Mrs. Nesbitt, my teacher, gave me a coat to wear. She had made it from one of her husband's old coats.

One evening, my teacher asked me to stay after school. She waited for the other kids to go home before giving me the coat. Mrs. Nesbitt didn't want me to be embarrassed in front of my classmates. The day I put that coat on, and felt the warmth all around me, I knew I was one lucky boy!

Mrs. Nesbitt was my teacher from the first grade through the eighth grade. I learned about the world around me in Mrs. Nesbitt's classroom. My teacher, God Bless her, even had to spank me a couple of times for fighting at school.

Even though we were in midst of Depression years, life seemed tranquil. These simple things I experienced as a child made life worth living.

John (age 10) at Coal Creek Valley School (Photo courtesy of John Inman)

CHAPTER FOUR
The Ute People

As children, we spent hours exploring the lands surrounding our farm. We found arrowheads, old stone tools and beads that once belonged to someone else. In school, we learned about these objects, and those who made them. I was fascinated with their story.

The hills and valleys where we lived had once been the traditional homelands of the Ute people. For centuries these mysterious Native Americans had depended entirely upon the land and its resources for their survival. The Ute were some of earliest inhabitants of the Colorado region. When the game they depended upon migrated with the seasons, so did the Ute.

Sadly, in the late 1850s, Ute homelands were in danger of being flooded by thousands of over-zealous miners and settlers. For decades, the Utes tried negotiating with the newcomers. Ouray, a Tabeguache Ute leader, and his wife Chipeta worked tirelessly to keep peace on behalf of the Ute people. In order to prove their friendship, the couple built a farm east of the lower Coal Creek Valley on lands given to them by the United States Government during the Brunot Treaty.

Petroglyphs in Shavano Valley. (Courtesy of Denver Public Library, Western History Collection, T. McKee, Call # Z-1282)

Chipeta and Ouray farmed the land and worked hard to show the government and the newcomers that the Ute were willing and able to live like "whites." Within several years, the couple's farm was flourishing! Still, non-Indians competed for the Ute homelands. Then, in 1879, a great tragedy struck.

Some White River Ute men had killed Agent Nathan Meeker at the White River Agency, after he had forced them to plow up their pony pastures. Meeker had even resorted to withholding food from the Ute people. He wanted them to give up their traditional customs and become farmers. The lands the White River Ute lived on made this difficult to do.

Major T. T. Thornburg and one hundred sixty of his troops headed toward the White River Agency. The Utes, fearful of being attacked, defended their lands. Within a few days, Major Thornburg and some of his top-ranking officers had been killed.

The White river Utes took Mrs. Meeker, her daughter Josephine, and Mrs. Price and her children hostage.

Site near the White River Agency in Meeker, Colorado.
(Courtesy of Vickie Leigh Krudwig)

Earliest photo of Chipeta and Ouray, 1860's
(Courtesy of Animas Museum, Durango, Colorado)

Chipeta and Ouray, along with several other Utes, and government officials helped rescue the hostages. Still, the Ute people were forced to leave Colorado.

Sadly, in 1880, just before the Ute were removed from Colorado, Ouray died. A heartbroken Chipeta, along with 1541 other Utes were forced from the lush, green Uncompahgre Valley, to the vast and desolate wastelands of northeastern Utah.

Once the Ute were relocated to the Uintah-Ouray Reservation, settlers quickly moved into the Ute domain, staking claims to the land. This included the lands in and around Montrose, and the area where we lived.

Even though the Utes were long gone, we children still found their arrowheads, scrapers and stone tools lying scattered across the valley floor and on the mesas. These ancient relics were fragile reminders of the Utes' long, proud existence in the Rocky Mountain region.

Sixty-seven years after the Utes removal from Colorado, our family was living off the very same lands that had supported them. I could almost feel their presence as I explored the hills and valleys near my home. Little did I know that I was about to make a startling discovery!

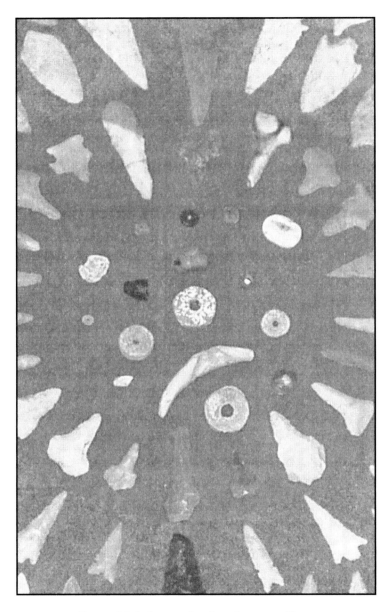

Some of John's arrowheads and stone artifacts.
(Courtesy of Vickie Leigh Krudwig)

CHAPTER FIVE
Buried Treasures

One day after school, when I was ~~eight~~ Six years old, I went out to feed the family's hogs. As usual, I had chores to do in the afternoon. I picked up the gray metal feed bucket and filled it with food. I walked up to the pen and began to call the hogs. I poured the slop into the wooden bin and watched as the pigs rushed past me and towards the food.

Those old pigs pushed their snouts deep into the trough. They grunted and groaned in pleasure as they gobbled up the tasty morsels. While the pigs ate, I leaned against a fence post and waited for them to finish. As the hogs ate their evening meal, I picked up a clump of dirt and threw it at an old gray stump. I smiled when I hit my target. I brushed the dirt off my hands and put them into the pockets of my overalls.

A well-hidden magpie scolded me from a nearby tree. I paused momentarily to study my surroundings while the hogs finished eating. The grassy hills of the Upper Coal Creek Valley seemed to wrap themselves around our homestead. I loved it when the afternoon sunlight filtered through the cool, white branches of the cottonwood trees. I could even see some of the old Ute trails ambling over the hills and down into the low-lying valleys near our farm.

My cousins and I loved hiking over those old Ute trails. We spent countless hours in search of adventure and treasures! We were delighted when we discovered arrowheads, scrapers and small glass beads lying in the dirt. My parents and teacher told me that these artifacts had been left behind by the Ute people, when they lived in our area. It thrilled me to think that Ute men, women and children may have lived on our lands at one time or another. Whenever older family members talked about the mysterious Ute people and their life in Colorado, I listened intently.

It was easy to imagine Ute teepees scattered across the valley while fearless Ute warriors rode their ponies across the land in search of game. I knew however, that the Tabeguache Ute people were long gone, never to

Painting owned by John Inmanm. Painting by Jack Daniel's..

return. The people had been placed onto reservations in Fort Duchesne, Utah. It bothered me to think that the lands in Utah were not like the rich, fertile regions of Montrose. Instead, the Ute had been put onto a vast and desolate land with very little water. Now, the Ute faced difficult times, too. That last thought made me sad for them. I sighed as I bent over to pick up the slop bucket. It was time for me to go inside.

As I made my way across the pen, I noticed that the pigs had gathered together. One of the pigs squealed as he pushed his snout deep into the soggy soil. It was typical for them, as they always looked for other things to eat. This time however, the pigs had rooted up some unusual objects. They weren't plants or stones. Curious, I picked up my bucket and headed toward the animals. I shooed the pigs away from the site so I could get a better look at their finds. The hogs grunted and squealed in protest as they trampled across the pen. What were the items, I wondered?

I set my bucket down and squatted to get a closer look. I poked one of the objects with my finger. It made of steel. I gripped the long cylinder and pulled hard. It made a sucking sound as I lifted the heavy object out of the ground. I couldn't believe it. I had found an old Navy 36 caliber ball-and-cap pistol! It was rusty after being buried for so long! I knew the gun was old, and I was thrilled with my find! I set the gun down inside my bucket.

Next, I pulled at the other object. It was smaller than the gun, and made of stone. Once I pulled the item out of the wallow, I wiped it clean with my finger, revealing a strange "L" shaped granite pipe. At first I thought it was part of the household plumbing. Yet after careful examination, I realized that it was a tobacco pipe. With the exception of a small chip on one of the corners, its brown, square bowl was smooth to the touch. There was no pipe stem, as it had probably rotted away in the wet soil. My heart pounded as I ran toward the house to show my find to the family.

Once I was inside, I cleaned and polished the old stone pipe. I carefully wrapped it in a scrap of fabric and put it into a empty blasting caps box. The orange tin box would keep the pipe safe from harm. Next I cleaned the mud off the rusty pistol. I put my treasures in my dresser drawer for safekeeping. That night, as I lay in bed, my mind was filled with all kinds of questions. How old was the gun and the pipe? Where had they come from? Who did they belong to originally?

CHAPTER SIX
The Mysterious Visitor

Several months after I found the stone pipe and the ball-and-cap pistol, a mysterious visitor came to the Coal Creek Valley School. I listened in amazement as he talked about his lifetime experiences. Doctor White had come to talk to us about Native Americans—especially his experiences at Fort Crawford just south of Montrose.

Fort Crawford had been built in the summer of 1880 at the request of the Tabeguache Ute leader, Ouray. Nearly 250 cavalry and infantry had come to help protect the Utes from encroaching settlers. Fort Crawford had proved ineffective. Non-Indians rushed to the Uncompahgre region when they learned that the Utes were being evicted from Colorado. Of course, I was thrilled as Dr. White described the life and early times of the Ute Indians.

I listened absorbedly as Dr. White described a skirmish that had taken place at a spring in the Coal Creek area long ago. "Many years ago," said Dr. White, "Shavano, a Tabeguache leader, and a small band of warriors from the White River Agency were on their way to see Chief Ouray at the Fort Crawford agency." The Doctor studied our faces

Shavano, (1869-1874) (Courtesy of Denver Public Library, Western History Collection, Wm. Henry Jackson, Call # WHJ-10327)

while he spoke. "The men had ridden from the Grand Mesa (near present-day Grand Junction) to Delta, where Ouray waited for them. The men carried with them a small stone pipe—the Ute Nation's peace pipe."

I leaned forward as Doctor White continued his story. "It was getting late and the riders were weary. They decided to camp near a small spring in the Upper Coal Creek Valley."

My mind raced! I could hardly believe what I was hearing. Were the doctor's words true? Could the pipe and the gun belong to the Ute people? I waited for the physician to tell the rest of the story.

"Shortly after Shavano and his men set up camp, they were attacked by another small band of Indians. A skirmish took place, and Shavano and his warriors fought to defend themselves. Shortly after the battle, Shavano realized that their sacred pipe was missing."

Doctor White looked up at the teacher and then into the faces of the children. I grew anxious. I could hardly wait for the doctor to continue his story. His face grew serious, and he paused for a moment. Then he began to speak. The words changed my world that day! I could hardly sit still!

Coal Creek Valley School #16.
(Courtesy of John Inman)

The stone peace pipe sits in John's hands. The wooden stem had rotted away in the wet soil. (Courtesy of John Inman).

"For several days, Shavano and his small band of Utes searched for the pipe. His efforts were in vain. The old peace pipe was lost forever. Shavano and his men returned to Delta without the peace pipe." Next, Doctor White began to describe the pipe. I could hardly believe my ears as he detailed its shape, size and the gray granite stone from which it was carved. The pipe, Doctor White said, had a small chip on one of its corners.

I remembered the day I found the pipe and gun in the hog wallow. Was it possible that my pipe was the very one Doctor White spoke of? When our speaker had finished his program, I stood up. I told Doctor White about the pipe and old rusty gun. I described the details of my discovery. Doctor White spoke excitedly, asking me if he could visit our home later on. I could tell that he was eager to see my treasures. The kids in my class were envious and I felt important.

When Doctor White arrived, my family gathered around him. I went into my room and opened my dresser drawer. I pulled out the rusty gun and the small tin box, which held the pipe. Doctor White waited anxiously for me to open the blasting caps box. I lifted the wrapped pipe bowl out of the box and unwrapped it. Doctor White's eyes widened in surprise. His face turned blissful as he picked up the pipe and examined it. The elderly gentleman ran his finger over the pipe bowl and to the chip on its corner. The pipe, he said, matched the description of Ouray's peace pipe perfectly!

The Doctor could hardly contain his excitement. He was convinced that I had indeed found Ouray's old pipe— the Ute Nation's peace pipe. "I will pay you fifty dollars for this pipe," said Doctor White. Everyone gasped. Fifty dollars was a lot of money to me, and to my family. We were still in the midst of the Great Depression. The money would come in handy, yet I wasn't quite sure what I should do. I almost accepted Doctor White's offer, yet something kept me from doing so.

My father was out of town working on the new Million Dollar Highway between Durango and Ouray. When he came home for the weekend, I told him all about Doctor White, the Ute pipe and the fifty dollars.

"Son, the pipe would be gone, and like a wisp of smoke, the money, too," said my father, "but do as you wish."

Nearly two weeks later, while I was out herding the neighbor's cows, Doctor White returned to our house. This time he brought the curator of the Denver Museum with him. Both men walked down the road to find me. They were anxious to see the pipe. By this time, the men had upped the price of the pipe to $100!

Both men were very disappointed when I refused their offer. The men turned to my mother. They hoped she would change my mind. Their plan did not work. I would not budge. Doctor White and the curator left our home without the pipe.

"I'm going to keep the pipe," I said to a disappointed Doctor White. I picked up the pipe and carefully wrapped it up. I put it back in its orange box. I decided then and there, that I would not sell the pipe to Doctor White or to the curator. Nor would I sell it to anyone else. I knew in my heart that my pipe was special, and that I should hold on to it. I vowed that I would always keep the pipe close to me.

CHAPTER SEVEN
The Simple Things in Life

In the fall of 1936, we were in for another move. Mr. McCombs, our landlord, bought another place in the lower Coal Creek area. The new owners had asked us to move. Mr. William Franklin, whom we called "Uncle Billy," came to our aid. Our family had always helped Uncle Bill with his seed onions, weeding, topping the seed and drying them. Whenever he needed help, he always came to our family first.

Uncle Billy bought the land that I live on today. Our family moved into the home and quickly settled down. For us Inman children, this meant we now had to walk more than two miles to and from school.

During the warmer weather, the walk was pleasant. Winters in the Coal Creek Valley, however, were fairly hard. We often had a difficult time navigating across the snowy landscape and through the drifts that covered the road. We often depended upon our neighbor's old sway back horse to help us. We would usually put the four youngest children on the horse, and the rest of us held on to her tail as she broke a trail through the snow.

After school, there were chores to do. My brothers and I cut wood and carried it to the house. Next, we watered and fed all the animals, including my mother's chickens. She raised up to two hundred of chickens each year. She'd sell the chickens to buy other things such as sugar, flour, coffee and other household necessities.

I remember these times with fondness. In addition to my mother's chickens, we had milk cows, horses, pigs, dogs, cats and a host of other "pets." My brother Bobby and I always had lots of strange pets around. We raised rabbits, pigeons and magpies.

Sometimes we would add a pheasant or two to our menagerie of creatures. When we cut hay in the nearby fields we would sometimes cut over a pheasant's nest. We would take the orphaned pheasant eggs home and put them under the hens that were setting at the time. The pheasants would hatch, and we would have pheasants roosting all around our property.

During the summer months, we sat on the lawn admiring our young prairie dogs while they scampered around in their cages. We made little harnesses for them and trained the prairie dogs to pull little sleds or wagons.

Like most boys in the area, we loved to go fishing too. We would hike up to Coal Creek and Spring Creek in hopes of catching fresh fish for supper!

These were relaxed times for my family. Our lives had finally settled down into a simple but pleasant routine. It seemed nothing could put a damper on our happiness

CHAPTER EIGHT
Keeper of the Pipe

In late spring, 1937, I began to have a lot of problems with my stomach. For a while I didn't tell anyone about the upset stomach or the sharp pains in my side. At night I would sneak outside and sit in the car, so I wouldn't disturb the others. I hoped the illness would pass. Unfortunately, it only worsened, and the pain in my belly was relentless. I had no choice but to tell my parents.

After some unsuccessful home remedies, I was taken into Montrose to visit with Doctor Lockwood. What was his diagnosis? Appendicitis! The Doctor explained that I would not be able to survive a trip to Denver for surgery, and I needed the treatment immediately. Doctor Lockwood talked to my parents. He would have to do the surgery at Mrs. Fender's Hospital in Montrose.

In the operating room, Doctor Lockwood began the surgery. My appendix was not in its normal position. It was too close to my liver. Doctor Lockwood said that I had a massive infection. The appendix had ruptured, yet the physician could not find the appendix. He cleaned up the abscessed tissue and washed me out with

This black and white drawing of Mrs. Anna Fender and her hospital was created to honor Mrs. Fender's tireless efforts to help the ill. (Sketch by Beth Atkinson, courtesy of Montrose Historical Society)

formaldehyde. Next he sprinkled sulfa powder into my wound, and added a drain.

Nature, said Doctor Lockwood, would have to take its course, as there were no antibiotics to help me fight the infection. There was nothing my parents or the doctor could do. My life lay in the hands of God. Doctor Lockwood, Mrs. Fender and my family and friends prayed fervently for a miracle to save me.

During my illness, my sister Elsie stayed close by my side. She had come to the hospital to help nurse me back to health. While I slept, Elsie helped Mrs. Fender with the cooking and other hospital chores. This would help pay for my medical expenses. The bill for my surgery was $95— more than my family could afford. My parents sent fresh fruits and vegetables from their farm in the valley, as well as poultry and dairy products. These were exchanged for the services the hospital provided – allowing my parents to honor their debt.

Of course, I was unaware of these details as I lingered between life and death. For 30 days I lay in my hospital bed, drifting in and out of consciousness. I was fighting for my life, while my worried parents and siblings watched over me. Elsie, too, stayed close. She rarely left my side, choosing to sleep in a bed close to mine.

During this difficult time, a man kept vigil by my bedside. He sat in the old wooden rocking chair at the foot of my bed. He rocked back and forth while I drifted in and out of consciousness. At first I did not recognize him, yet I found comfort in his presence. At one point he spoke to me. Suddenly I knew who he was. It was the famous Ute leader, Chief Ouray! The man studied me with his dark almond eyes, and his long black braids hung down over his shoulders. He nodded and acknowledged me.

Ouray told me that he kept his vigil in order to keep the evil ones from taking over my body and soul. He also told me that I would live to be an old man. I was to be "Keeper of the Pipe." When I was old, he said, there would be an event when I would return the peace pipe to the Ute people. He told me a golden eagle would help the people. This was to be a sign of healing of the Ute Nation and the non-Indians that they might live in harmony.

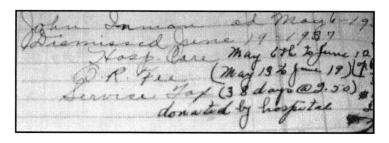

Journal Entry from Mrs. Fender's Hospital at Montrose Histrorical Society. (Courtesy of Vickie Leigh Krudwig)

Chief Ouray, 1880, posing for a Washington, D. C. photographer shortly after the Meeker Incident. (Courtesy of Denver Public Library, Western History Collection, Walker Art Studio, Call# Z-31584)

When Ouray finished speaking, I lay back on my pillows. Deep within myself, I knew what I had to do. I would take good care of the pipe, and when the time was right, I would honor Ouray's wishes and return the pipe to its rightful owners.

Finally after three long months, I was released from Mrs. Fender's hospital. I was glad to be able to go home and grateful to be alive.

Later on, Elsie told me that she had seen the wooden rocking chair move back and forth. She thought a breeze had moved it. Elsie said she quietly walked over to the chair and put her hand on it to stop its motion. When it was stilled, Elsie turned her attention to me. She smoothed the covers over my frail body, and tucked them snugly around me. When she turned around she could hardly believe her eyes. The chair was again rocking by itself. It moved effortlessly as if someone were sitting in it. Yet she saw no one sitting there.

Elsie stopped the chair again. Goosebumps covered her arms and legs. She said she couldn't get over the fact that the chair continued to rock by itself. She said that it was as if someone had been in the room with us. Little did she know that I could see the famous Ute leader, Ouray sitting in the chair.

When I got home, I took my pipe out of the drawer, and out of its orange tin box. I studied it for a while, and vowed that I would never let the pipe out of my possession. I would never sell it. I would not fail Ouray, or the Ute people.

John just before his release from Mrs. Fender's, 1937
(Photo courtesy of John Inman)

Elsie and her husband, William (Bill) Roy. Bill's grandmother was a Southern Ute from New Mexico.

John, one year after his hospitalization.
(Courtesy of John Inman)

CHAPTER NINE
World War II

In the fall of 1940, just three years after my brush with death, I started classes at the high school in Montrose. I stayed with my Uncle Robert and his wife for the first half of the school year. When their daughter came home from college, I was forced to move to a small, one room cottage behind Macy's Grocery Store on West Main Street in Montrose. I lived there for the rest of the year.

The following year, I moved in with my sister Elsie and her new husband, William Roy. He was manager at the old Monell Ranch in the southern part of Montrose— now the site of the Montrose golf course. I helped him feed the dairy cows and pigs, and put up hay for my keep at their home.

During my junior year in high school, I stayed at the old Belvedere Hotel, where I worked as a night clerk. At night, when there was little to do, I would drive down to the Train Depot to meet the train when it came in. There I would pick up passengers and take them back to the hotel.

Early each morning I would clean "clinkers" out of the furnace, and reload it with coal. I wanted to be sure that the black coal furnace was full so that there would be

John's graduation from Coal Creek Valley School
(Photo courtesy of John Inman)

plenty of heat and hot water for our guests. My room at the Belvedere was located just behind the desk for the guests' convenience. In exchange for my services, I received a small salary plus my own room.

Mr. Sanders, the owner of the Belvedere, had a son who had enlisted into the service. Therefore, I was given the opportunity to work and live at the hotel. I was lucky; I was able to attend high school. Many of us "country kids" did whatever was necessary in order to go to high school. There were no busses available, so we had to find ways to live and support ourselves within the city of Montrose.

By 1941, when I was just fifteen, the United States entered World War II. Over 138,000 men and women from Colorado alone had enlisted, or were drafted into the armed services. During this turbulent time, many of the enlisted men and women had lost their lives. In addition, the entire country was experiences shortages of gasoline, sugar and

The Belvedere Hotel (1920) where John worked. (Courtesy of Denver Public Library, Western History Collection, W. Torrance, Call # Z-7403)

John just before shipping out.
(Photo courtesy of John Inman)

tires. Ration stamps were issued for these precious commodities. It was difficult to buy tires for our vehicles.

Shortly after I turned 18, on July 4, 1943, I was inducted into the United States Army. In August I packed my bags and headed east, riding the train, all expenses paid, to Flora, Mississippi, where I was stationed at the Mississippi Ordinance Plant. For six weeks, I spent my days in the classroom learning how to fill out forms and other official paperwork, while also learning how to operate the equipment that the Ordinance Department handled.

Once my training in Mississippi was complete, I was commissioned to go to Fort Ord, California. On the way I stopped over in Colorado. I was given a twenty-one day leave so I could visit with friends and family before being shipped out.

Even during wartime, I kept my promise to Ouray and to the Ute people. I took the pipe, still in its protective tin box, with me. I kept it in a small "ditty" bag with my razor, tooth brush and other personal items.

After a short stay in Fort Ord, California, it was time to ship out. Under the cover of darkness, the troops were taken down river to Richmond, where we would board a ship. There were nearly 5,000 of us crammed onto the "Presidential Lines Ship." The passenger ship had been converted into carrier and renamed the "U. S. S. Grant."

In the wee dark hours of morning we reached the outer limits of San Francisco Bay. There were no lights on, no radio contact and no flags on the masts. We were careful not to give away our position. No one tossed their cigarette butts overboard either. We had to be cautious, as we were on our own. There was no convoy to follow us either.

Everyone on board had jobs to do, as there was only a skeleton crew of Navy personnel. I was placed on gun crew #21 badge. During the day I got a lot of practice on

*House at Baguio near Camp John Hay used on weekends
and for temporary duty. (Courtesy of John Inman)*

the guns. We often shot at debris floating in the ocean. I loved nighttime best. I was allowed to sleep on deck, and got to go to the front of the chow line when it was time to eat! We ate beans three times a day.

The trip across the ocean was a long one. It took us 45 days to reach Leyte, in the Philippines. We had zigzagged across the equator five times. At one point, during the night we had to lay silent on the ocean. A submarine had been following us for three days. Shortly after that, the captain of our ship died unexpectedly from a massive heart attack. We cruised into New Guinea and waited offshore for five days, while the government brought in another captain.

Finally, a sea plane landed with our new captain on board. The pilots picked up the body of our captain, which we had stored in the meat locker. Once again under the cover of darkness, we sailed on to Sidney, Australia. Once there we refueled, and re-supplied our ship fresh water and provisions. We picked up 14 soldiers who had been hospitalized there. These men would return to their units stationed in the Philippines.

Monsoon season had gripped the Philippines when we arrived. We dropped anchor and tried to make the best of it. Of the 5,000 men on our ship, only 1,000 of us disembarked in Leyte. We were put to work immediately. Large trucks carrying supplies were stuck in the mud. We spent three days unloading them. Much to our dismay, the trucks were carrying the bodies of our fellow soldiers.

Our base was next to the American Military Cemetery. For three days we carried our fallen comrades on stretchers through knee high mud and water to the cemetery. At first, the smell of the decomposing bodies was so over powering, it made us sick. Then we grew accustomed to the stench. I wanted to get this job done quickly. This was my first real "taste" of what war was all about. It was a real shocker for this young man, who had only lived in Montrose, Colorado.

Ships and Barges (also called ducks) in the Lingayan Gulf.

Base "M" headquarters shortly after a typhoon.
(Courtesy of John Inman)

Due to the conditions, many men became sick. One of our troops developed spinal meningitis. Our unit was quarantined for few days, and later we had to get immunizations to keep us healthy.

Finally after about two weeks, new orders came. I was one of 32 men called out. We packed our bags, drew our rations and gathered up our allotment of cigarettes. We were headed north towards the Lingayen Gulf. We boarded a PT boat at night, and headed toward Corrigenda. Seventeen men, in addition to 14 others we had picked up in Sidney, Australia, disembarked.

Four of us were assigned to the 226th Ordnance Base Headquarters. When we stepped onto the dock at Corrigenda, a 4X4 waited to take us to the base. We were given two days to get settled and to catch up on some badly needed rest. On the third day after arrival, we reported to duty. After checking in with the Commanding General, I was appointed as the new Sergeant Major of the Ordnance Depot, and 1st Sergeant of the Headquarters

Detachment. The old Sergeant was being transferred to another location. Needless to say, I was amazed. You might even say I was "numb." After all, I was only a "Tech 3rd Grade," and I was going to be giving orders to higher ranking troops. Although I was nervous about my new role, the Commanding Officer assured me that everything would be alright.

I worked at the Ordnance Depot for nearly two years. The United States was now beginning to push toward Japan. I had been transferred to Base M Headquarters duty at the 226th Ordnance Depot. While I was there, the base received the prestigious Presidential Meritious Award. Shortly after that, I was awarded my Captain's Bars. I was now the officer of Port Ordnance. I picked a new Sergeant Major. He was my Chief Clerk and had proven himself repeatedly.

With my new promotion came more responsibility. The pay was the same, but there were other benefits. I received my own room, had an office at the dock, and best of all, I was allowed to eat aboard the Merchant Seaman's Ships with the Captains. We ate like kings! We had steak, lobster and lots of fresh veggies—a far cry from beans!

On Aug. 6, 1945, the atom bomb was dropped on Hiroshima, Japan. The stunned officials of the Japanese government surrendered. The war was over and rotations to send our troops home began. In 1946, I was given orders to go home. I carefully packed my bags, and checked to be sure my pipe was snug in its orange tin box. The pipe had gone around the world with me. It had become an indelible part of me, bringing me comfort during the difficulty of wartime.

Many times when my mind was cluttered or I had decisions to make, I would slip off for a moment of solitude. I would carefully remove the pipe from its container and hold it my hand. I'd immediately grow calm and my mind would become clear. I made my decisions with certainty.

Perhaps, I thought, some of the spiritual wisdom from Ouray and the other Ute leaders, who once held the pipe and smoked it, still lingered within its granite bowl. It was as if these long gone ancestors were with me in the throes of battle, and in the quiet moments, too. Now the pipe and I were headed home to the United States to begin a new life.

On the way home, I was fortunate enough to be put in charge of one compartment of the ship. I had my own air-conditioned room, and my duties were simple. I did roll call each morning, and checked on the welfare of the troops. If anyone was ill, I made sure they were put on sick call. I would issue the orders for the day. This included details such as shower schedules, and what hours the men could be on deck.

CHAPTER TEN
Home Sweet Home

Our trip from Manila, Luzon Philippines to San Francisco took only one week. As soon as I arrived, I took leave and visited San Francisco while completing my orders for discharge. There I met my aunt, uncle, cousins and younger brother, Bobby Gene. Bobby, a member of the United States Navy had just arrived at port and I was glad to see him.

Sadly, a few years after his return, my brother Bobby was diagnosed with cancer. He had been present at the atomic bomb testing site in Bikini, Atoll. Then he and countless other troops had returned home on one of the contaminated ships used to carry the materials for the atom bomb. The malady later killed him. I missed Bobby Gene, as he was my dating, hunting and fishing buddy while we were growing up.

I returned home with an honorable discharge in my hand and a letter signed by President Harry S. Truman. I had thirty days of pay in my pocket when I stepped off the bus in Montrose. There were no crowds or family members to greet me. They were unaware that I had finally made it

***After World War II, John and his brother Bobby Gene recon-
nected in San Fransisco, Californa. (Courtesy of John Inman)***

home. Telephones were still not widespread; in fact, we had just gotten electricity just before I left home for the service.

Luckily, I located someone I knew, and he gave me a ride to the Coal Creek Valley. At home I fell into the arms of my mother, father and siblings. Most of the troops I knew had come home in this quiet, unassuming way. There were no parades or yellow ribbons. We simply slipped quietly into the life stream, trying to readjust to peacetime conditions at home. We also faced unemployment, as there were many more men looking for work, and fewer farms to employ them. Some of our acquaintances weren't even aware that we had been gone to war, or that we were lucky enough to come back.

In 1947, the state of Colorado gave its veterans $20 a week for 52 weeks (also called "52-20"). This would help us financially while we resettled ourselves.

A neighbor in Shavano Valley offered me 30 acres of his farm land in hopes that I would share crop and plant beans on the property. This neighbor was working in the Idarado Mine to make extra income to keep up with the payments on his farm. I was grateful that he had a job to make that possible!

After two flash floods, hail storms and tons of weeds, I had my first harvest that year! After planting the entire 30 acres, I ended up with six 50 pound bags of beans. I kept one bag and gave the remaining five to the farm owner.

In 1948, I worked for different farmers by doing "piece work"—this included weeding onions, putting up hay, or whatever else the farmer requested. I earned anywhere from $1.00 to $2.50 a day, plus meals. In the late fall, I topped onions, picked potatoes and helped harvest ripe peaches in Palisade, Colorado. Later that year, I decided it was time for me to seek better employment.

Uncle Billy's root cellar.
(Courtesy of Vickie Leigh Krudwig)

I took off in my 1941 Pontiac in search of jobs with my mother, brother, brother-in-law and youngest sister. My brother-in-law had relatives working at the lumber mills at Coos Bay, Oregon. He said that the jobs were plenty there. When we arrived, we were disappointed. Out of the entire group, I was the only one who was offered a job, primarily because of my status as a veteran. I scaled trees and measured them for timber.

Our family knew that we could not make ends meet on my salary alone. We packed up the car again and this time headed south toward San Francisco. My aunt, uncle and cousins were living there. Within two days, I went to work for the Swift and Company. I remained with that company for more than 19 years.

During that time, I began to have stomach troubles. The familiar pain associated with my appendicitis reared its ugly head. I had no choice but to visit a friend's Doctor. After lots of x-rays and a host of other medical tests, Doctor Brooks said I needed an operation. He insisted that I wait to have my surgery, as there was a United States doctor's convention taking place soon. I would not only receive care from the best doctors in the United States, it would cost me nothing! There would be no doctor bills or hospital fees.

Shortly after the convention began, I had my surgery. My unusual anatomy and my ruptured appendix had caused a large part of my bowel to harden. Even though Doctor Lockwood had never located my appendix, he had hoped that the body would take it upon itself to heal. The new surgeon however, was forced to remove the damaged section and reattach the small bowel to the large bowel. The results were successful and I only missed one month of work. Though Doctor Brooks had promised there were no medical bills, there was a catch. My entire surgery was filmed for use in the classroom to help train medical students.

It seems like the years flew by after the war. I tried my hand at several things before finally settling down in the Coal Creek Valley, west of Montrose. I had the opportunity to fly airplanes, race boats and enlist in the reserves with 141st Marine Fighter Squadron. I worked a variety of jobs in Arizona, Utah and Denver over the next 18 years. Wherever I traveled and whatever I did, the Ute pipe was part of my life.

I was grateful for the opportunity to be a part of long past history by finding the old stone pipe. It had become a source of comfort to me through the years. Never did I realize that the pipe would impact my life so greatly.

My life has never been the same, as I learned how to slow down and take time to remember the past. Not just mine, but the times when Native Americans lived off of the lands. One of my favorite memories is exploring the ancient Anasazi ruins in the southwest. There were times when I sat among those ruins, cooled by a gentle breeze. In those quiet moments, I could almost hear the sounds of the ancestors' voices as the children played, and the people went about their daily business.

Still, I recalled the words of the great Ute leader, Ouray: *"There would be an event when I would return the pipe to the Ute people."* I couldn't help wondering when that time might be.

CHAPTER ELEVEN
A Time to Let Go

In 1994, I heard the dreaded word – cancer! The word came from the doctor standing across from me. I had recently retired from my job at a local mine. I had returned to Montrose in hopes of settling down. I had plans to live on the lands I had grown up on in the Upper Coal Creek Valley. Yet the words spoken filled me with doubt. I was diagnosed with colon cancer, and the hideous disease had eaten its way through my intestines and wrapped itself around my back bone. Without surgery, the prognosis was grim.

Still, I needed time to think. I spent two weeks trying to decide when and where I would have my surgery, as there were several options. Needless to say, I stayed close to Montrose, the homeland of Ouray and his wife, Chipeta. I had my surgery and then endured a year of chemotherapy treatments. I had survived! Here I am, I thought!

As I recovered, I began to sense that the time had come for me to return the pipe to the Ute people. It was time for the healing to begin. I took the box containing the pipe and I put it in my pocket. The Delta Council Tree Pow

Sillouettes of three of the four golden eagles.
(Courtesy of John Inman)

Wow was underway, and representatives from all three Ute nations were there. I wondered if this would be the place and the time.

I stood in the crowd and watched as the dancers in fine regalia danced to the beat of the large hide drums. I studied the faces of the individuals, hoping for a sign. Somehow, from deep inside, I knew that this was neither the time nor place. There was too much money being exchanged and I felt a sense of greed. I put my hand in my pocket and touched the pipe. Perhaps another day, I thought.

Then, in 1998, the signs that I had waited for had finally come. The Ute Indian Museum in Montrose was being rededicated to the people. Chipeta, a great woman and wife to Ouray, and her brother, John McCook, lay buried on the grounds of the museum—at Ouray Memorial Park. People from all three tribes would be present at the dedication. I knew without a doubt that the time had come for me to relinquish my guardianship of the pipe.

On Sept. 27, 1997 in a humble, but powerful ceremony, the old granite pipe was rightfully returned to the Ute people. Representatives from all three tribes were present to receive the pipe on behalf of the Ute Indian Museum. The return of the pipe signified the fulfillment of my obligation to Ouray and to the Ute people.

Nearly 73 years have passed since I first found the Ute peace pipe. I had just finished working on my life's story on the eve of Sept. 21, 2004. On the following morning, a mother golden eagle and her three young eaglets swooped out of the sky and into my yard. The hair on the back of my neck stood up, as I recalled Ouray's words in my hospital room in 1937. He said there would be a golden eagle to help the people heal. These magnificent birds stayed close to my home for nearly two hours. They were not disturbed when I stepped outside to take pictures and get a closer look.

Then, without warning, the graceful birds lifted effortlessly into the air. I watched in awe as the four of them spiraled in a circle, soaring higher and higher each time. It was as if to say that the circle of my long and amazing journey had been completed. Perhaps this is true, and perhaps there is more to come.

Fourth golden eagle sits on another pole near John's house.

The spirit of the Ute People is alive and well at the Chipeta Day Celebration, August 2004. (Courtesy of Vickie Leigh Krudwig)

ABOUT
JOHN INMAN

John Inman was born in Heber City, Arkansas. In 1928, John and his family moved to the Upper Coal Creek Valley, in Montrose, Colorado, where he lives today. John is an avid history buff. On September 27, 1997, John returned the Ute pipe to the Ute Indian Museum, marking the end of his guardianship of the pipe.

Because of World War II, John was unable to complete his high school requirements, and did not graduate. In 2000, John fulfilled his dream and graduated from Montrose High School with full honors.

John holds the ball and cap pistol he found when he was a boy. (Courtesy of Vickie Leigh Krudwig)

ABOUT CO-AUTHOR, VICKIE LEIGH KRUDWIG

Vickie is a native of Colorado. She lives in Denver, Colorado with her three children, and her husband, Mark. Like John, Vickie is passionate about history, and specifically, Colorado's amazing past. She met John Inman during a trip to Montrose, in 2001. There Vickie had come to research her newest books, Searching for Chipeta — The Story of a Ute and her People, and We Are the Noochew— A Brief History of the Ute People and their Colorado Connection. It was then that Vickie learned about John's extraordinary experiences after finding the Ute pipe in a hog wallow near his home.

In addition to her books, Cucumber Soup, Hiking Through Colorado History, We are the Noochew, Searching for Chipeta, Wings Above the Water—A Fisherman's Legacy, Cats, Dogs, Bugs, and Frogs, Taming the Tornado Tube, numerous illustrations and articles created by Vickie have been published nationally and internationally Her stories have appeared in *Highlights for Children Magazine*, *Kid City Magazine*, *Wild Outdoor World*, and in local newspapers.

BIBLIOGRAPHY

Bougue, Linda - *The Memoirs of Flying Horse Mollie a Yampa Ute*. Montrose, Western Reflections, 2001

Decker, Peter R. - *The Utes Must Go*. Golden, Fulcrum Publishing, 2004

Emmitt, Robert - *The Last War Trail*. Boulder, University Press of Colorado, 2000

Krudwig, Vickie Leigh - *Hiking Through Colorado History*. Englewood, Westcliffe Publishers, 1999

Krudwig, Vickie Leigh - *Searching for Chipeta*. Golden, Fulcrum Publishing, 2004

Krudwig, Vickie Leigh - *We Are the Noochew*. Federal Heights, Juniper Winds Press, 2004

Marsh, Charles M. - *People of the Shining Mountains*. Boulder, Pruett Publishing Co, 1982

Rockwell, Wilson - *The Utes a Forgotten People*. Ouray, Western Reflections, 1998

Simmons, Virginia Connell - *The Ute Indians*. Boulder, University Press of Colorado, 2001

Smith, Anne M. - *Ethnography of the Northern Utes— Papers in Anthropology No. 17*. New Mexico, Museum of New Mexico Press, 1974

Utley, Robert M. - *The Indian Frontier of the American West*. New Mexico, University of New Mexico Press, 1989